A Guide To Making Skincare Formulas

Victor V. Barber

Introduction

This is a comprehensive resource that takes readers on a journey through the world of skincare formulation. It covers a wide range of topics to equip beginners with the knowledge and skills needed to create effective skincare products.

The guide starts with an exploration of the anatomy of the skin, delving into the functions of the epidermis, dermis, and hypodermis. It highlights the relationship between skin anatomy and achieving healthy, glowing skin, setting the foundation for understanding skincare at a deeper level.

Holistic skincare is introduced, emphasizing the importance of identifying different skin types, including oily, dry, combination, normal, sensitive, and dehydrated skin. Each skin type is thoroughly explained, along with signs and treatment plans to address specific concerns. Common skin ailments like acne, melasma, and stretch marks are also discussed, providing diagnostics and treatment plans.

Understanding a skincare regimen is crucial, and the guide breaks down the Cleansing-Toning-Moisturizing (CTM) routine for various skin types. It explains exfoliation and the different types of hydroxy acids (BHAs and PHAs) used for skincare. Readers learn how to choose the right exfoliator and create a regimen schedule tailored to their needs.

The guide dives into cosmetics ingredient review, offering insights into ingredient data sheets and the mixing and synergy of cosmetic ingredients. It covers the classification of cosmetic ingredients, beginner equipment used in skincare formulation, and good manufacturing practices, ensuring safe and effective formulation.

Measurement and conversion of units are essential skills in skincare formulation, and the guide provides detailed information on preventing errors during measurement. It also covers the conversion of units and the measurement of concentration, making it easier for beginners to work with ingredients effectively.

Preservation of skincare products is a critical aspect of formulation, and the guide explores antioxidants, preservatives, and chelating agents. It explains antimicrobial efficacy tests and challenge tests, ensuring that skincare products remain safe and free from contaminants.

In summary, this book is a comprehensive and informative resource that covers the essentials of skincare formulation. It empowers beginners to understand skin anatomy, identify skin types, create effective skincare regimens, work with cosmetic ingredients, and ensure product preservation. With this guide, aspiring skincare formulators can embark on their journey with confidence, knowing they have a solid foundation of knowledge and skills.

Contents

CHAPTER ONE

1.0 ANATOMY OF THE SKIN

1.1 The Skin as a Body Organ

The skin is the largest organ of the body. It serves as a protective barrier against microorganisms and injuries from the environment. The skin has different texture for the different parts of the body, for example; the skin is thinnest around the eye and hardest on the soles of the feet followed by the palms. The human skin is composed of three layers.

a. Epidermis
b.   Dermis
c.   Hypodermis

Epidermis: This is the outermost layer of the skin that is visible. It is used to determine the skin type, skin health and skin tone or colour. This epidermal layer is constantly renewed every day. The epidermis is of the utmost concern to a skincare therapist.

Function of Epidermis

i.   Houses new and dead cells: New cells formed from the hypodermis move to the epidermis and the new cells replace the old cells in the epidermis, leaving the old cells to flake off. As we age the frequency of old dead cell removal reduces. Exfoliators and scrubs are used to accelerate the shredding of old skin cells.

ii.   Protects the Skin: Epidermis is made up of skin protein known as Keratin. Keratin gives the skin its toughness and strength by

adhering cells to each other. It keeps the skin moisturised by trapping
water and provides a waterproof barrier between the environment and the inner organs; therefore, the first treatment plan for a therapist is to repair the skin barrier protection of the epidermis.

iii.   Regulates our skin tone/colour: Epidermis houses melanocytes.

Melanocytes are responsible for production of the skin pigment

vii

'melanin'. The amount of melanin transferred to the epidermis determines the colour of the skin.

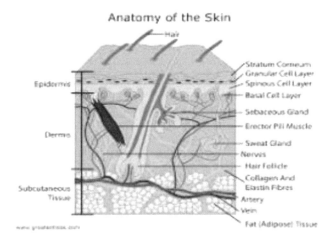

Image 1: The three layers of the skin

Source: Google Image

Dermis: The dermis is directly underneath the epidermis. It is the thickest layer of the skin. The dermis houses the hair follicles, connective tissues, blood vessels, oil and sweat glands, and other fibrous and elastic tissues.

Function of Dermis

i. The major function of the dermis is to provide strength and flexibility to the skin via collagen and elastin synthesis. These two fibres combine to provide structure to the skin. As we age the amount of collagen synthesised diminish leading to sagging skin and wrinkles.

ii. It promotes sweat creation in response to environmental temperature. The sweat helps to cool the body to maintain uniform body temperature.

3

iii.   It secretes sebum which keeps the epidermis moist and healthy and also prevents passage of pathogens.

iv.   Hair follicles in the dermis produce hair around the body.

v.   Blood vessels in the dermis carry nutrients and oxygenated blood to epidermis. It also discards waste products.

Hypodermis: Hypodermis is also called the subcutaneous tissue because it is beneath the skin. It is the layer of the skin that provides plumpness. For example, women have their highest percentage of subcutaneous tissue in thighs and buttock as compared to men whose shoulders have highest hypodermis.

Function of Hypodermis

i.   The major function is the storage of fats.

ii.   It also helps to give balance.

iii.   It supports the upper dermis and epidermis layer and serves as a connector of the skin to bones and cartilages.

iv.   It acts as a temperature regulator for the body and protector against heat and cold as well as sweat.

1.2 Relationship between Skin Anatomy and Glowing Skin

Aging: The epidermis houses lots of water which is sealed by keratin and it also houses sebum which serves as natural skin moisturiser. As we age, the strength potential of keratin weakens making moisture loss rapid. To compensate for loss of moisture, the dermis synthesises more sebum to serve as moisturiser and increase moisture retainment. Excess sebum secretion leads to pores clogging and blockage of dead cells. Poor dead cell shredding leads to dull skin and closed comedo. Also, collagen synthesis diminishes as we age.

So, to combat aging, we must always replace lost moisture by increasing hydration. Exfoliate regularly using mild exfoliants that will not distort keratin, to artificially remove dead cells and clogged pores.

3

Also as we age, it is necessary to use products that boost collagen synthesis such as vitamin C and avoid products that strip the skin of collagen, moisture and sebum such as astringents and physical abrasive shrubs.

Skin Colour: Since melanocytes areproduced in the basal dermis layer and transferred to the surface epidermis, to regulate melanin production and colour, melanocytes cell transfer and/or synthesis must be inhibited in the dermis. In order to achieve melanocyte inhibition, the product must be able to penetrate deep to the basal dermis. Any attempt to use products that only peel the surface keratinocyte cells in the epidermis leads to destruction of the protective function of the epidermis keratinand consequentlyskin protective barrier is compromised to give a sick skin.

Skin Health/Glow: To achieve a healthy skin, the skin must be pampered by hydration to prevent moisture loss. A hydrated skin leads to reduction in sebum production and a balanced skin barrier is maintained. Also, mild chemical exfoliation must be used to remove dead cells to allow appearance of new cells. Lastly, skincare products especially leave on such as serum and moisturisers should contain ingredients that boost collagen and keratin synthesis and infuse hydration.

In summary, to remain ageless with glowing skin, you have to top up hydration, boost collagen, protect keratin, and remove dead cells.

3

CHAPTER TWO

2.0 HOLISTIC SKINCARE

2.1 Introduction to Skin Care

The first step to treating skin ailments and formulating a suitable skincare product for a client is to know your customers' skin type and skin condition if any. This requires a series of questioning and using the answer to cross-match the signs and symptoms for the different skin types and common skin conditions.

2.2 Identification of Skin Types

There are basically four types of skin:

a. Oily b. Dry
c.   Combination
d. Normal

These skin types are mostly evident on the face, however dry skin may also be found in the entire skin.

2.2.1 Oily Skin

Persons with oily skin have visible oil on their face. An oily skin houses excess sebum. The sebum produced leads to clogged pores. The most successful way to naturally maintain an oily skin is via sebum regulation using exfoliators such as salicylic acid to remove excess sebum and intense hydration. Intense hydration signals the sebaceous cell to reduce sebum production because the skin protection barrier is functional hence much sebum is not needed.

3

Signs of Oily Skin

The face is shiny at all times, such that when you touch the face you will get oil, no matter how small. Persons with oily faces usually have large pores and acne.

2.2.2 Dry Skin

It is the opposite of oily skin. The skin looks dry, as if one rubbed talc powder. I call it "harmattan skin". The skin lacks sebum. In almost all cases of dry skin, the skin also lacks water because there is no sufficient sebum to help seal in moisture. Dry skin is best treated by incorporating products that have fattening effect such as shea butter, coconut oil and other emollients and occlusive. Intense hydration also helps.

Signs of Dry Skin

The skin looks dry and dull. Person with dry skin may experience itching, scales, wrinkles and stings.

2.2.3 Combination Skin

Persons with combination skin have both oily skin and dry or normal skin type. However, when treating this skin type we first determine if it is oily/dry or oily/normal. If it is oil/normal, we treat it as oily skin. If it is oil/dry, we treat it as both oil and dry interchangeable. When treating alternatively always look out for the skin type that is more dominant.

Signs of Combination Skin

Combination skin types have oily T Zone (forehead, nose and

cheeks). Chin and jaw are dry or normal.

3

2.2.4 Normal Skin

This is the perfect skin with just the right amount of sebum (neither oily or dry).

Signs of Normal Skin

They do not have acne, large pores, flakes or itching. They can use any product and still look great. Persons with normal skin type are advised to stay off harsh chemical products, so they do not change their skin type.

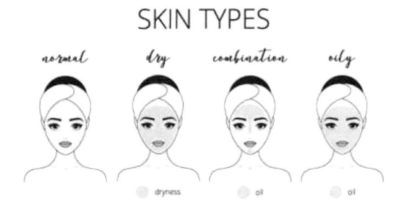

Image 2: Signs of the different skin types

Source: Google Image

3

2.3 Identification of Skin Conditions

Persons with any of the above skin types may have one or both of the following skin condition:

a. Sensitive skin

b. Dehydrated skin

The following skin conditions usually refer to the entire skin but more dominant on the face. However, there are few exceptions.

2.3.1 Sensitive Skin

This refers to skin that is highly reactive to chemical products and weather/environment. Sensitive skin gets irritated easily. Sensitive skin may be hereditary or may be as a result of extreme weathers (hot or cold), or low air humidity. Also, sensitive skin may arise due to destruction of the epidermal layer, usually as a result of harsh chemicals and improper use of exfoliators.

Signs of Sensitive Skin

Sensitive skin is prone to inflammation such as rashes and bumps. Most skincare products sting or burn the face. The face may be flaky with dry patches, redness and breaks out easily. Persons with sensitive skin are sensitive to UV rays and bad weather such as winter.

Treatment Plan for Sensitive Skin

While it is almost impossible to totally treat sensitive skin using the right products may help alleviate the condition. Products with soothing ingredients such as calendula, aloe, chamomile and allantoin can be used to reduce skin irritation. Also, fragrance and essential oil free products are more suitable. It is advisable to use products that have ceramides, hyaluronic acid and aloe vera to help restore the protective function of the epidermis. As advised by WebMD, beauty products with alcohol, sulphates, and benzoyl peroxides should be

3

avoided and retinoids should be used with caution. I personally recommend soap free bath gels for persons with sensitive skin.

2.3.2 Dehydrated Skin

This is mostly a temporary skin condition caused by lack of water in the epidermis. When the skin protective barrier is damaged, the skin can no longer retain water. Most of the time, dehydrated skin may experience excess sebum production as a compensation to replace keratin deficiency. This phenomenon is often confused with the development of oily skin. And most times, treatment is misdirected by attempting to reduce sebum using drying agents such as exfoliators. This results in further production of more sebum as compensation for reduced sebum and the circle continues further increasing dehydration.

Signs of Dehydrated Skin

The most obvious sign of dehydrated skin is a wrinkled skin. A common test of dehydration is to "take a small portion of the skin around the cheeks and squeeze it lightly. If you notice any wrinkling and the skin do not bounce back after you let go, then the skin is dehydrated".

Treatment Plan for Dehydrated Skin

Hydration is the solution to dehydrated skin. To treat skin dehydration, maintain a regimen that contains a lot of humectants. Example using a glycerine soap or better still a non-soap bath gel with hyaluronic acid, glycols and sodium lactate. Tone using rosewater in humectants such as hyaluronic acid, glycerine, lactic acid and stabilised aloe vera gel. Use an aqueous based moisturizer. Finally, lock in moisture using a moisturizer, emollient

or occlusive suitable for the skin type.
3

2.4 Common Skin Ailments Diagnostics and Treatment Plan

2.4.1 Eczema

Eczema is a common skin condition in children but may also affect adults. It is an inflammatory skin disorder with itchy, cracked and rough patches that may have blisters.

There is no established treatment protocol. However, symptoms can be relieved using a triple action cream with corticosteroid, antibacterial and antifungal topical cream. This cream should not be used beyond 3 weeks. Other skin care routine that relieves eczema are:

a. Bath with lukewarm water.

b. Apply lots of humectants and lock in moisture using a rich occlusive.

c. Repair skin barrier.

d. Wear breathable clothing such as cotton.

e. Avoid astringents. Use mild soap or preferable non-soap cleansers.

f. Do not scratch.

g. Avoid sudden temperature change and activities that cause sweating.

h. Follow up triple action cream with non-steroidal anti-inflammatory creams rich in botanical extracts and phenolic hydrosols.

2.4.2 Acne

Acne is also an inflammatory skin disorder which may be infected by bacteria or fungi causing pus filled inflammation. It is a temporary skin disorder that can be treated using deep skin exfoliants, sebum regulators and antibacterial or antifungal. The treatment plan depends on the type of acne. All treatment must be followed up with intense hydration and skin barrier repair because active ingredients such as salicylic acid, benzoyl peroxide, retinoid and glycolic acid commonly used to treat acne have drying and dehydrating side effects.

3

2.4.3 Melasma

Melasma is a symmetrical brownish discoloration that is mostly common among dark skinned females (Fitzpatrick III-VI). It occurs mostly on the face and other areas exposed to UV ray (sunlight) such as the neck and forearm. The two major causes of melasma are: UV ray from sun and hormonal imbalance. Melasma caused by hormones do fade off on their own once hormones (estrogen and progesterone) are balanced. For example pregnancy and birth control induced melasma.

Sun induced melisma needs to be treated. Unfortunately, most cases of treated melasma reoccur, therefore continuous follow up are needed when treating melasma. Treatment plan include the following;

a. Daily use of sunscreen SPF 50 irrespective of weather condition. b. Wearing a wide brim hat to provide additional sun protection.

c. Use of lightening, anti-inflammatory and cell turn over exfoliating ingredients to fade discoloration. Examples are:
Azelaic
acid, tretinoin, chemical peels, corticosteroid and hydroquinone.

d. Intense hydration should be added to treatment to strengthen skin health and allow speed up of skin cell turnover.

2.4.4 Stretch Mark

Stretch marks are permanent scarring of the skin due to

stretching of epidermis and dermis to reveal the fatty hypodermis. This explains why stretch marks are often found in fatty areas of the skin such as stomach, breast, thighs etc. Early scaring appears as a reddish/purplish lesion. As the skin heals, the marks turn into a whitish/silver colour with no fibrous structure that is soft to touch.

Factors that cause stretching of the dermis are rapid growth and hormonal changes caused by puberty, pregnancy, oral and topical steroid use. The use of topical steroid cream for skin blanching is the major cause of stretch marks among young girls in Africa.

It is unfortunate that once stretching of the dermis has occurred it is

3

impossible to totally reverse dermis pliability because the fibroblast has lost its ability to produce collagen and elastin fibres. Treatment plan involves an attempt to fade off scars using lightening ingredients such as glycolic acid, also use of topical ingredients that allow rapid cell turnover such as tretinion, microdermabrasion and laser treatment may reduce appearance of scar.

3

CHAPTER THREE

3.0 UNDERSTANDING SKIN CARE REGIMEN

3.1 Building a Skin Regimen

Regimen is the beauty routine we follow to give flawless skin. Most skin regimens are however centred on the face. The regimen you choose for a client depends on their skin type. We have:

3step regimen- Cleanse. Tone, Moisturize (CTM)

5step regimen- Cleanse. Tone, Moisturize, Exfoliate, Mask

It is good to follow a strict regimen that works for you at least CTM. For example you will not get the real benefit of a hydrating cleanser if you do not follow up with a hydrating moisturiser.

3.2 CTM for Oily Skin

Cleansing Oily Skin

Persons with oily skin benefit from a two stage cleansing regimen. The first cleansing called the pre-cleanse step. Pre-cleansing is used to hydrate/moisturize the skin to help stabilize the skin barrier. A healthy skin barrier is less likely to produce excess sebum. Three types of pre cleansing exist:

a. Honey Pre-cleansing: This involves massaging honey into the face a few minutes before cleansing.

b. Micellar Water Pre-cleansing: Micellar water is applied with the aid of a cotton pad in a circular, upward motion just before cleansing.

The use of micellar water for pre cleansing is especially beneficial to persons with oily and dehydrated skin.

c. Oil Pre-cleansing: Non-comedogenic and hypoallergenic emulsified oil is used. They are commonly called deep cleansing oil.

3

Few drops of the oil is applied on the face and gently massaged into the face just before cleansing. Oil cleanser is most beneficial at night. It is used to remove greasy makeup and sunscreen to prevent pores clogging.

After pre-cleansing, cleansing can be done using soap free face wash. Persons with oily skin are strongly advised not to use caustic soap because they do not have the ability to properly emulsify with oil leaving the skin clogged. For persons with acne, you might consider acne face washes containing salicylic acid or benzoyl peroxide.

Toning Oily Skin

Toning is most important for persons with oily skin. Toners formulated for oily skin should be used; it should have ingredients that fight excess oil such as alpha hydroxy acids (AHAs), green tea, apple cider vinegar (ACV). For persons with sensitive skin, rose water toner with additives can be used. Toners may be applied with the aid of a cotton pad or spritz using a spray bottle.

Moisturizing Oily Skin

Oily skin mostly benefits from oil free moisturizers or gel based moisturizers. My personal opinion is "to use gel moisturizers and serum/light weight oil (argan, grape seed, olive or jojoba) and use emulsions sparingly.

Why?

"Oily skin already has an excess production of oil, this means it does not really need a moisturizer, what it needs is hydration. Hydration helps to keep the skin barrier and lipid level balanced, hence the need for face gels". However, use of lightweight oils (2-3) drops will help lock in moisture preventing evaporation. Also, presence of oil on the skin helps deceive the skin no to produce more sebum. The skin produces sebum when it feels that more oil is needed.

3

3.3 CTM for Dry Skin

Cleansing Dry Skin

Dry skin is a bit tricky to cleanse because cleansing naturally strips the skin of oil. To prevent further drying, I advise the use of honey for AM (morning) cleansing and creamy face cleanser for PM cleansing. Adding a few drops of light weight oil into bath water is encouraged.

It is advised to use face wash specially formulated for dry skin. Watch out for ingredients such as; cocoa butter, glycerine, shea butter, oils and wax. Persons with dry skin should avoid taking hot showers and limit face steaming.

Toning Dry Skin

Toning dry skin is a great way to introduce oils and humectants. Toner containing 1-2% glycerine in rosewater is great for dry skin. If treating for itching and irritation, infuse rose water with chamomile tea or flowers. You can also add other humectants such as glycols, propanediols, lactate et al.

Moisturizing Dry Skin

Two step moisturizing is advised for persons with dry

skin. Why?

Often, people with extreme dry also have dehydrated skin. So it is advised to treat skin for both dryness and dehydration.

So, after toning, use a humectant such as; hyaluronic acid serum, apply stabilized aloe vera gel (alcohol free), snail mucin or any aqueous moisturiser. Massage into damp skin and leave for a few minutes. Then apply oil, body butter or any heavy moisturizer.

3

3.4 CTM for Combination Skin

Combination skin means we have to cater for both oily and dry skin. Combination skin is difficult to deal with. So this is my suggestion. First determine if the skin is oilier than treat as oily or more dry then treat as dry. If not sure, in the morning treat it as oily and at night treat it as dry.

When cleansing combination skin. In the morning, use a hydrating face wash for oily skin and at night use a cream face wash for dry skin.

Toning combination skin means we need to find a balance between oil and dry skin. Witch hazel and lactic acid toners are great for this skin type alternatively rosewater may suffice.

Moisturizing combination skin, just as cleansing, means we use gels in the morning and oils at night.

A normal skin type can benefit from any of the regimen meant for other skin types.

3.5 Exfoliation

Exfoliation is an act of removing old dead skin from the epidermis using physical or fruit acids. It involves breakdown of peptide bonds that link keratin in epidermis, making them to fall off and revealing new active keratin. It can be used to solve several skin conditions such as: sunburn, post inflammatory hyperpigmentation, skin lightening et al. It is important to note that a healthy skin does not need exfoliation regimen. Naturally, the skin exfoliates itself, however certain factors such as age and dehydration may slow down exfoliation, hence the need for assisted exfoliation.

Physical exfoliation comes in the form of scrubs, brushes and dermabrasion. Because this process uses mechanical force to break

3

peptide bonds, it is not suitable for persons with dry skin, sensitive skin, acne prone skin, large pores or any inflammatory skin condition such as eczema. This reason is the skin can easily get micro tears during scrubbing further escalating existing skin condition. Also, physical exfoliation does not have the ability to penetrate the inner epidermis stratum to unclog pores.

Chemical exfoliation on the other hand can be used by problematic skin. The type used depends on the skin condition and intended use. See Table 1 as a guide.

3.5.1 Types of Chemical Exfoliators Chemical

exfoliators can be grouped under three types: **Alpha**

Hydroxy Acids (AHAs)

AHAs are water soluble acids that exfoliate the surface of the skin to improve texture. Examples are; lactic acid, glycolic acid, malic acid, citric acid, tartaric acid and mandelic acid. They are used as exfoliants at concentrations of 3-5%. Higher concentration above 10% is regarded as chemical peel which must be administered under the supervision of a dermatologist.

Beta Hydroxy Acids (BHAs)

BHAs are oil soluble acids so they have the ability to penetrate deeper into the epidermis via the pores. So, they exfoliate the surface epidermis and the inner dermis layer of the skin. BHAs are therefore used to unclog pores, reduce sebum and improve skin texture. Example is: salicylic acid. Salicylic acid is commonly used at a concentration of 2%.

Poly Hydroxy Acids (PHAs)

PHAs are water soluble acids that function in a similar way as AHAs. The major difference between AHAs and PHAs is the larger molecular size of PHAs which limits their ability to penetrate the skin [3] making them surface exfoliators. Their large molecular size also makes them less irritating and suitable for sensitive skin. Findings also show that PHAs have antioxidant and hydrating properties. Examples are: gluconolactone and lactobionic acid.

3.5.2 Choosing the Right Exfoliator

The type of exfoliator used will depend on skin type and skin condition if any. Persons with normal skin type can use both physical and chemical exfoliators. However, salicylic acid should be used with caution to prevent sebum in balance.

Persons with oily, acne prone, rosacea and sensitive skin will benefit from using salicylic acid while dry skin will benefit more from AHAs. Almost all skin types can use PHAs. For more specific skin conditions and choice of exfoliants, use Table 1 as a guide.

As a rule of thumb, exfoliation should be followed with rich moisturizer and adequate sun protection.

3

Table 1: Chemical exfoliants used for different skin conditions

	AZ	CA	CT	GA	GAL	GY	LA	LAB	MA	MAN	RE	SA	TA
Acne	X		X			X			X	X	X	X	
Combo	X					X	X	X	X	X		X	
Dark spots	X	X	X			X	X	X	X	X	X	X	X
Dry	X			X	X	X	X	X	X	X			X
Ingrown hairs						X	X					X	
Mature	X	X	X	X	X	X	X	X	X	X	X		X
Oily	X		X			X		X	X	X	X	X	
Scarring	X	X				X			X		X	X	
Sensitive	X			X	X		X	X		X			
Sun damage	X	X	X			X	X		X	X	X		X

Key: AZ- Azelaic: CA- Carbolic: CT- Citric: GA- Galactose: GAL- Gluconolactone: GY- Glycolic: LA- Lactic: LAB- Lacto-bionic: MA- Malic: MAN- Mandelic: RE- Retinoic: SA- Salicylic: TA- Tartaric

X means acid allowed

Source: Healthline

3

3.6 Mask

Facial masks are used to deliver nutrients without evaporation or extract toxins from skin. The mask may cover the entire face or be customized to suit a specific area of the face such as; forehead, nose, chin/jaw or patches (pimple patches). The type of mask will depend on skin type and skin need. They can be used for short periods such as clay masks or long periods such as sleep masks. It is important to follow the user guide when using a face mask.

Irrespective of the type of mask used, a mask must be applied on a clean face and a manufacturer's instruction on how long the mask should stay on the face should be included in the label.

3.6.1 Types of Mask

Clay Mask: Clay masks are mostly made from muddy clay. Common examples of clay used are: bentonite and kaolin. They are primarily used for extracting toxins from oil, acne prone face to give a deep cleansing effect. They may be combined with other deep cleansing agents such as activated charcoal. It is advised not to leave a clay mask for too long on the face to prevent reverse osmosis effect.

Peel-Off Mask: Peel off mask as the name implies are applied to the face, left for a specific period of time according to manufacturer's instruction and peeled off the face. They are used to provide light exfoliation during peel off for oil and acne prone skin. They are also used for pores unclogging and hyperpigmentation. Due to abrasion during peel off, persons with sensitive and irritant skin are advised not to use a peel off mask.

Charcoal Mask: Charcoal masks are made from activated charcoal. They provide excellent absorption properties and can be used to draw out impurities, dirt and sebum from the skin. Charcoal masks can be customized to suit different skin types. Persons with oily skin will benefit from a charcoal-clay combination while persons with dry skin can use a charcoal mask with oils, butter and humectants.

3

Sleep Mask: Sleep masks are overnight masks used to deliver intense hydration and moisturising. They come in the form of cream for dry skin and gels for oily skin. Sleep masks are packed with ingredients to ease specific skincare concerns such as brightening, acne, anti-aging, moisturizing. It is advised to apply a sleep mask as the last step of skin care routine.

Sheet Mask: Sheet masks are made from fabrics such as: non-woven fibre, cotton, hydrogel and bio-cellulose. They can be made to cover up the face or target specific high need areas. The fibres are soaked in concentrated serums meant to deliver targeted needs. They are mostly used for moisturising and hydrating and not exfoliating. So, it is common to see ingredients like aloe vera, hyaluronic acid and vitamins as active ingredients. They are mostly left on the face for 20-

30 minutes before removing. However, just like other face masks, it is best to follow manufacturers' instructions. For extra benefit, a

moisturizer should be applied on a sheet mask to reduce evaporation

effect especially for sheet mask made from cotton and non-woven fibre.

3.7 Regimen Schedule

Now you have figured out how to help clients build the routine to follow daily in order to achieve a flawless skin, the next step is to draw out a regimen schedule to enable easy traceability of what to do daily. Figure 2 shows an example of a 5 step regimen schedule.

Note, this is not a typical schedule, the steps can change based on skin needs but as we can see in the schedule, CTM is daily and toning step can be swapped with use of serums or essence. Also, the skincare schedule can be further broken down to morning and evening.

3

SKINCARE CALENDAR

MONDAY	CLEANSE + TONE + MOISTURIZE
TUESDAY	CLEANSE + MASK + TONE + MOISTURIZE
WEDNESDAY	CLEANSE + EXFOLIATE + SERUM + + MOISTURIZE
THURSDAY	CLEANSE + TONE + MOISTURIZE
FRIDAY	CLEANSE + MASK + SERUM +
SATURDAY	CLEANSE + TONE + SERUM + + MOISTURIZE
SUNDAY	CLEANSE + EXFOLIATE + SERUM + + MOISTURIZE

Image 3: Skincare Regimen Schedule

Source: Pinterest

3

CHAPTER FOUR

4.0 COSMETICS INGREDIENT REVIEW

The first step in any cosmetics product formulation including skincare is an in depth research study that is aimed at spelling out and documenting the reason behind the recipe creation. You must decide what solution the cosmetics product provides and how it differs from existing products. Some questions that can lead to this answer are:

a. Who is my target market?

b. What are the top existing products that are similar to my product and target market?

c. How do I make my product unique from other existing products?

d. What are the basic ingredients needed?

e. What are the active ingredients needed to make my product unique?

After these questions have been answered and ingredients identified, each ingredient must be listed separately for cosmetics ingredient review.

3

4.1 What is Cosmetics Ingredient Review?

It is an act of studying a cosmetics ingredient information data sheet to understand the function of the ingredient. It answers the following questions.

Why the ingredient is added.

When the ingredient is to be added.

How the ingredient should be added.

What quantity of ingredients should be added.

It also answers questions like:

How can the ingredient be preserved?

Are there any better or cheaper alternative ingredients?

Does the ingredient have any synergistic or antagonistic effect with other ingredients in the recipe?

Are there any safety regulations regarding the ingredient?

The most important knowledge any skincare formulator must have is the ability to build a recipe from the scratch. This requires the knowledge of the function of each of the ingredients that makes up a recipe. The knowledge of ingredient review also helps to review and improve existing DIY 'do it yourself' and standard recipes to suit your customer needs. Without a deep

understanding of why we add ingredients to a formulation we can be misguided by so many false and incomplete recipes widely available online.
3

4.2 Ingredient Data Sheet

It is also called a product data sheet (PDS) or safety data sheet (SDS). It is a fact sheet that provides all the information you need to know about an ingredient and its synergy and interaction with other ingredients in a recipe. An ingredient data sheet should contain the following information among others.

1. Full common name and chemical name of the ingredient.
2. Physical properties for identification.
3. Usage percentage range and maximum recommended concentration.
4. pH stability.
5. Temperature of mixing.
6. Solubility or mixing phase.
7. Uses and Benefits.
8. Synergistic and antagonistic effect with other ingredients if available.
9. Safety profile.

The above information should be provided by the ingredients supplier. However, further research is needed using peer reviewed articles to authenticate supplier ingredients data sheets. This information serves as a guide to a formulator to help decide on what percentage to add, at what stage of production it should be added, how to solubilize the ingredient and pH of the final

product needed to stabilize and preserve the ingredient.
3

Table 2: Example of Information Data Sheet

Common Name: Vitamin C

Chemical Name: L-ascorbic acid

Description: Active form of vitamin C as it occurs naturally. 100% pure (USP/FCC grade). pH 3 (0.5 % solution). White powder, ultrafine and odourless. Easily soluble in water & alcohol

INCI Name: L-ascorbic acid

Benefits:

- Potent antioxidant (shown to be able to protect skin from oxidative damages)
- Can improve appearance of aged and fragile skin
- Widely used as add-on ingredient in skin-lightening products to correct hyperpigmentation and age spots
- Antioxidant effect can be increased by combining L-ascorbic acid with L-ascorbyl palmitate and/or vitamin E

Use: Add to water phase of formula, usual final concentration 0.5-10
%. Tip: sprinkle vitamin C powder slowly to the water under constant stirring to assure that everything dissolves completely. Should be formulated at pH 3-5 for best results. For external use
only.

Safety: GRAS

Applications: Lotions, creams, sun care & after sun products, shampoos, makeup products (e.g. lipsticks).

Source: Making Cosmetics
3

From the information data sheet of vitamin C, we can deduce the common name, chemical name, physical properties, solubility, usage concentration, phase mixing, pH stability, synergistic effect with vitamin E, uses, benefits and safety profile.

So from this information sheet above, if you come across a glow oil using vitamin C as an active ingredient you can categorically say the vitamin C is not active or it's a false claim because your ingredient research on vitamin C says it is not soluble in lipids.

The next question becomes are there any other alternatives? This brings us to the next area of ingredient review.

4.3 Alternative Ingredient

Just like in culinary science, cosmetics science has numerous ingredients that perform the same functions. These ingredients have different solubility, pH and temperature stability. It is therefore the duty of the formulator to determine the best available alternative. In doing all this, Google is your friend, especially Google Scholar.

Back to vitamin C oil, since vitamin C is water soluble, we use an oil soluble derivative such as ascorbyl palmitate. We also research its efficacy compared to vitamin C and how to increase its efficacy.

In a nutshell until you have put together all this information, it is wrong to skip the ingredient review phase no matter how appealing a recipe is.

3

Table 3: Ingredient Information Data Sheet Template

Common Name:	**Chemical Name:**
Colour:	**Solubility:**
Usage range (%):	
pH stability:	**Phase Mixing:**
Uses/Benefits:	
Application:	
Alternative ingredients:	
Synergy ingredient:	
Safety Profile:	

Use Table 3 as a template to start your cosmetics ingredient review journey. If you need more guidance, I will be happy to hear from you using any of the contact information provided in the "Conclusion Page".

3

4.4 Mixing and Synergy of Cosmetics Ingredients

Cosmetics ingredients can be broadly classified into: water, emulsifiers, moisturizers, thickeners, preservatives, colours and fragrances. It is important to note ingredients of similar classification are most likely soluble in each other. However, there are exemptions especially among actives. So, in formulation they are grouped together. The act of mixing similar cosmetics ingredients together is known as **Phase Mixing**. So when you see a standard recipe, they are grouped into phases according to their similar classification.

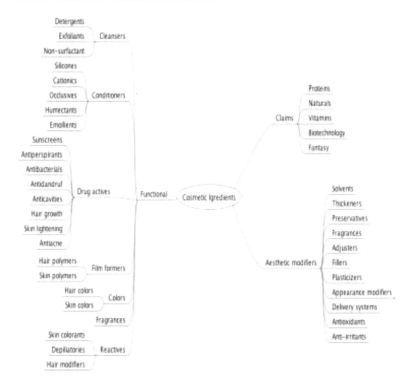

Image 4: Classification of cosmetics ingredients

3

The biggest mistake a young formulator can make is to ignore this knowledge of phase mixing. Mixing ingredients randomly leads to unstable and immiscible products.

4.4.1 Types of Phases in Cosmetics Formulation

Aqueous Phase: This phase contains all heat stable ingredients that are soluble in water.

Oil Phase: This phase contains all heat stable ingredients that are soluble in oil.

Cool down Phase: Any ingredient added at temperature below

40°C.

There are some special ingredients that do not mix in any of these phases. It is your duty to note their solubility and temperature stability during your cosmetics ingredient review. So, use the solvent the ingredient is soluble in to dissolve it. Also determine if the ingredient dissolves in a hot or cold solvent. Lastly, after dissolving, you must choose which phase the ingredient best fits, i.e. dissolved ingredients can be added during cool down or in the aqueous or oil phase.

4.4.2 Specific Information when Mixing Ingredients

a.   For emulsion such as creams, lotions, creamy mask and other emulsion that contains at least 50% water, always use oil soluble emulsifiers (w/o) with hydrophilic-lipophilic balance (HLB) of 3-10 and always add water to oil.
b. When making products that contain less than 10% of oil such as cleanser, aqueous toner/serum or essential oil in aqueous

medium always use solubilizers (o/w emulsifiers). Blend oil in solubilizer (1:3 – 1:8). Add solubilised oil to water.

c. Ensure oil and aqueous phase are in the same temperature before mixing together.

d. Actives should be added in the cool down phase except otherwise stated.

3

e.   The preservative you choose will depend on the pH of the final product.

f.   Ensure that all actives added are stable within the pH of the final product.

4.5 Classification of Cosmetics Ingredient

Water: Water usually makes up the bulk of most cosmetics ingredients. It is used to dissolve most ingredients and provide consistency to emulsion. Water used must be distilled water, free from microbes, toxins and particulates. It is sometimes called Aqua. For increased skin benefits, water can be enriched with herbs to produce herbal water and hydrosols. Hydrosols and herbal water can be used to replace distilled water in formulations.

Emulsifiers: Emulsifiers are ingredients used to prevent other ingredients that do not mix together (oil and water) from separating. They usually consist of a hydrophobic (oil soluble) and hydrophilic (water soluble) end. This allows them to reduce surface tension of oil and water mixture, to create a homogenous product. Examples of emulsifiers are: waxes, fatty acids, fatty alcohols and partial glycerides.

A subclass of emulsifiers are solubilizers, they also have similar properties as emulsifiers however, they are more water soluble with HLB of 13 -18. Also, the final product formulated is more translucent and transparent due to the smaller particle size of the dispersed phase.

Moisturizer: Moisturizers are used to give cosmetics a creamy, silky feel. They also serve as water proof to seal up ingredients (occlusive) or as thickener to increase bulk size. Moisturizers can be broadly classified into: occlusive, humectants, emollients and thickeners.

Occlusives: They act as waterproof. They are used to trap water in the skin increasing skin water content. They can be greasy such as oils, butters, mineral oil and petroleum jelly or non-greasy

3

such as dimethicone and other silicone derivatives. Choosing the right occlusive is important to prevent clogged pores. Persons with oily skin type are advised to use non-comedogenic occlusives (lightweight oils or non-greasy occlusive). Occlusives are best applied on damp skin.

Humectants: Humectants are used to attract water from the dermis to the epidermis. They are also used to attract water from the atmosphere especially when the weather is humid (>70% humidity). Examples of humectants includes; glycerine, glycols, hyaluronic acid, sodium lactate, sorbitol and lactic acid. For best result, occlusive should be used after a humectant to help prevent evaporation of trapped water.

Emollients: Emollients are cosmetics ingredients used to give the skin a soft smooth and pliable appearance. They consist of occlusive, humectants and even emulsifiers. They help fill the skin crevices for a slip feeling. They are often known as the skin lubricant.

Thickeners: Thickeners are used to give cosmetic products bulk size in order to increase product consistency. Most thickeners also provide some level of emollient properties. Examples of thickeners includes; fatty acids, waxes, triglycerides, gums, mineral clays and hydrolysed starch.

Preservatives: Preservatives are essential ingredients needed in cosmetics formulation that contains water or formulation with pH within the range of 5-8. They are used to increase cosmetics shelf life and prevent microbial growth that can spoil cosmetics and possibly harm users. Preservative must be water soluble. The type of preservative used depends on the pH of the final product. They are usually added in the cool down phase. Examples of common preservatives are: benzoates, sorbates, parabens, organic acids and formaldehyde releasing agents.

Colour: Colour can be natural or synthetic substance used to give colouring to finished cosmetics products. It also provides aesthetic appeal and to give a shimmering effect. Common natural colouring tinclude: beet powder, turmeric, cochineal insect and henna. Synthetic colouring includes; mica and iron oxides. Colours may be classified as: dye and pigments. Dyes are water soluble and pigments

3

are dispersible in oils.

Fragrance: Fragrances are used to give pleasant smell to products. Market research has shown that fragrances can be used to influence customers' decision to purchase a product. Essential oils are steam distilled fragrances gotten from aromatic herbs. Essential oils are gaining more attention in natural skincare formulation because of added advantage of therapeutic effect, as a result of high percentage of phenolic compounds. Most scented cosmetics product contains combination of fragrance and/or essential oils. Examples include; myrrh, lavender oil, sandalwood oil, citrus oil and musk. Fragrances are mostly added at the cool down phase of formulation.

4.6 Beginner Equipment used in Skincare Formulation

a.   Stick/Immersion blender: Used in homogenising ingredients during formulation.

b. Scales (in g and in kg): Two types of scales are needed. A small

digital scale that measures in grams up to 300g with ±0.01 accuracy and another that allows measurement in kilogrammes with ±1g accuracy.

c.   pH reader: A pH meter can be used for more accurate measurement of pH or for estimated measure, a universal pH strip

will suffice.

d.   Thermometer: It is used to measure the temperature of cosmetic formulation. Mercury in glass thermometers is commonly used. For increased accuracy, the thermometer should have a temperature range of 0-100^{0}C.

e.   Volumetric measurement: Beakers, bowls and volumetric flask of ranging volumes are needed.

f.   Disposable Pipette: Allow measurement of small volumes in drop wise, increasing accuracy.

g.   Stirring rods, Spoons and Spatula: For manual mixing and measuring of ingredients.

h.   Glass Funnel: For aseptic packaging of bottleneck containers.

3

i.   Gloves: Gloves are used to protect you from hazardous ingredients and protect the formulation from you (cross contamination).

j.   Eyewear/Goggles: When working with high levels of fumes such as concentrated acids and alkali, it is important to safeguard the

eyes.

k. Dehydrator: It is used for uniform drying of herbs and other fresh ingredients needed to be converted to powder. However, if unavailable, powdered herbs can be bought from organic sellers.

l.   Coffee Grinder: It is used to pulverise herbs and grains.

m. Crock Pot: Used as a slow cooker for hot oil infusions, herbal water and hot soap making.

n.   High speed mixer: For shear mixing of ingredients and to aerate body butters.

o.   Soap mould: Soup mould is used to give desired shape to bar soaps. It can be made from wood, metal or silicone materials.

3

CHAPTER FIVE

5.0 GOOD MANUFACTURING PRACTICES IN SKIN CARE FORMULATION

5.1 Good Manufacturing Practices

Good manufacturing practices (GMP) are practical steps used to ensure the reproduction and quality of the manufacturing process of skincare products. It cuts across all sections of manufacturing. GMP cuts across raw materials, premises, equipment, personnel, manufacturing, packaging and storage.

5.1.1 Raw Materials

It is important to purchase quality uncontaminated materials that meet set standards. This can be achieved by requesting for a SDS that shows the concentration of possible contaminants is within acceptable limits. In countries where SDS is not well regulated, the solution could be purchasing raw materials from trusted and verifiable sources.

Water used for skincare formulation must be microbes and heavy metals free. Distilled water is the most preferred option. Chelating agents such as EDTA and phytic acid can be used to reduce free heavy metals in distilled water.

5.1.2   Premises

The environment used for production of cosmetics must be sanitized and disinfected.

Sanitisation involves the removal of physical dirt, particles and dust from surfaces using brooms and wipes.

Disinfection involves the removal of pathogenic microorganisms from working areas/surfaces.

3

Two common disinfectants are used by small and medium scale (SMEs) cosmetics companies.

Bleach (10%): Bleach disinfectant is produced by mixing 10% sodium hypochlorite with 90% distilled water.

Alcohol (70%): Alcohol disinfectant is produced by mixing 70% ethanol or isopropyl alcohol with 30% of distilled water.

Disinfectants can be rubbed on a clean surface by the aid of cotton wool or sprayed around the working area and environment.

5.1.3 Equipment

Equipment just like premises must be disinfected. For ease of disinfecting, glass and stainless steel materials should be used for small scale manual production while stainless steel should be used for machineries. Equipment must be cleaned with soap and detergent, rinsed with water and sterilised. The most used method of sterilisation for SMEs is **Wet Steaming.** Autoclave is used for wet steaming. In the absence of an autoclave, pressure pot can be used. For automated machineries, consult the user manual on cleaning and sterilisation procedure.

For other equipment that is heat sensitive, alcohol or bleach can be used to disinfect equipment after washing. However, it is important to note that disinfection only removes pathogenic bacteria.

5.1.4 Personnel

Personnel are formulators and other ad hoc staff that have direct contact with raw materials and finished products. Optimal hygiene must be carried out by all personnel to prevent cross contamination.

Cross contamination can be prevented by:

a. Regular hand washing.

b. Use of disposable gloves during formulation and handling of raw materials and finished products.

3

c. Constant disinfection of the work area.

d.   When formulating cream, lotions and other microbial susceptible cosmetics, use of nose mask and head tie/cap is important.

5.1.5   Manufacturing

The manufacturing stage is the most important step in GMP. During manufacturing, it is important to be conscious of cross contamination from equipment, premises and personnel.

The best advice I can offer is "during manufacturing, prevent distraction or acts that make one pause production for other activities". Regular use of hand sanitizer or disinfectants during production also helps. Lastly, always clean and sterilise/disinfect the work area and equipment before manufacturing commences and use a disposable glove that must be changed when non production acts have been performed.

5.1.6   Packaging

The most common packaging materials used in skincare are plastic, glass and steel. All packaging materials must be washed and disinfected. Re contamination should be prevented after disinfection.

After production, the hygiene kept during manufacturing must be maintained during packaging and sealing.

5.1.7   Storage

Finished products should be stored in a clean, cool, dry and dark place to prevent recontamination from dust and also oxidation and microbial growth due to unfavourable environmental factors such as light, heat and moisture.

3

CHAPTER SIX

6.0 MEASUREMENT OF INGREDIENTS

The ability to accurately reproduce a recipe is the dream of every formulator. Errors in measurement can have very drastic consequences in skin care formulation. Apart from inconsistency in delivering quality products to customers, deviation from recommended usage of most active ingredients may lead to skin damage.

6.1 Types of Errors in Measurement

Systematic Error: These are reproducible inaccurate measurements. It is caused by poor understanding of unit conversion and calculation of concentration. It means a formulator continuously uses the wrong percentage in a recipe.

For example an ingredient needs 2% to be active and a formulator always adds 1%, causing the product to be inactive.

Random Error: Random error means the formulator does not have the know-how to take the same measurement repeatedly resulting in random numbers. This error is most common in formulators that use volumetric measurement such as measuring cups and measuring spoons.

For example, an ingredient needs 1% to be active and 2% leads to irritation. A formulator sometimes uses the tip of a spoon to get 1% other times 2% and other times 0.7%, leading to inconsistency in quality.

3

6.2 How to Prevent Errors during Measurement

a. The only accurate instrument for measuring ingredients is a SCALE. The measurement should be within the range of the scale. It is therefore advised to have two scales. A scale that allows measurement of small quantities in grams, and another scale that measures large quantities in kilograms.

b. There should be a set standard variation allowed during measurement to prevent random error.

c. The scale must be auto zeroed after each measurement.

d. All units must be harmonised and converted to percentage.

e. All calculations should be properly documented before measurement commences.

f. Ensure personnel taking measurement are well trained.

6.3 Conversion of Units

The accepted S.I unit for measuring ingredients is grams for small quantity (g) or kilogram for large quantity (kg). Therefore, all recipes in millilitres, ounces, cups and spoons must be converted to grams or kilograms.

To convert volumetric measurement like ounce and millilitres to weight (g or kg), use the formula below (equation 1)

$$Weight = Density \, X \, Volume$$

$Weight = Density \, X \, Volume$ **Equation 1**

So before you start your calculation you have to find out the density of the ingredient to be converted.

Example 1: If you have a recipe that measured ethanol in volume (100 ml), you will Google the density of ethanol and impute the figures using the formulae above.

Weight = 0.789 X 100 = 78.9g

Note: Density of ethanol is 0.789

3

So, instead of measuring 100ml, you have to weigh out 78.9g and failure to do this will lead to gross systematic error of 21.1.

If ingredients are in cups and spoons the easiest way will be to directly weigh the content in these containers after subtracting the weight of the empty container.

It is important to note that most recipes online that use units outside grams and kilograms are not from professionals that understand the effect of errors in making quality skincare. So, these recipes should not be trusted.

6.4 Percentage and Product Replication

As explained earlier, ingredients are measured in grams/kilograms (g/kg) using a scale. But when writing down formulations, g/kg must be converted to either g or kg to allow uniformity. The choice depends on the quantity of the majority of ingredients. If more than
70% of ingredients are below 1kg, then g is chosen as preferred unit, while if majority of ingredients are in kg, the ingredients in g are converted to kg.

Then the g or kg will be further converted to percentage (%). The reason for using percentage is to allow ease of recipe multiplication. Each percentage equals 100g. Before each batch formulation, the percentage is reconverted to g or kg for ease of weighing.

Conversion of g to kg

$$1000g = 1kg$$

$$1000g = 1kg \hspace{5cm} \textbf{Equation 2}$$

Conversion of kg to g

$1kg = 0.001g 1kg = 0.001g$

3

Equation 3

Conversion of weight (g/kg) to percentage (%)

Percentage =   Weight of Ingredient   X   100

Total Weight of all ingredients **Equation   4**

Conversion of percentage (%) to weight (g/kg)

Weight =   Percentage X Batch Size

100   **Equation 5**

Example 2

To formulate body butter, the following ingredients were copied online. The formulator intends to make 1kg (1000g) of butter using the ingredients below.

Ingredients

Shea butter	60g
Cocoa butter	50g
Mango butter	40g
Moringa oil	30g
Neem oil	20g
Grape seed oil 100g	

Solution 2

First we notice that all measurements have been converted to weight in g. Gram is used because all ingredients are in small quantities below 1kg.

3

For each ingredient we will calculate the percentage using equation 4

Percentage = Ingredient X 100 = Weight of

Total Weight of all ingredients

Shea butter (%) = 60/300 X 100 = 20% Coco

butter (%) = 50/300 X 100 = 16.7% Mango

butter (%) =40/300 X 100 = 13.3% Moringa

oil (%) = 30 /300 X 100 = 10% Neem oil (%)

= 20/300 X 100 = 6.7%

Grape seed oil (%) = 100/300 X 100 = 33.3%

Ingredients Recipe (g) batch size 1000	Percentage (%)	Final Recipe for (g)
Shea butter 60g	20%	200g
Cocoa butter 50g	16.7%	167g
Mango butter 40g	13.3%	133g

Moringa oil	30g	10%	100g	
Neem oil	20g	6.7%	67g	
Grape seed oil		100g	33.3%	333g
Total Weight		**300g**	**100%**	**1000g**

3

The first step is to convert the grams to percentage and from the percentage we can easily multiply the recipe. In this example, all ingredients were converted to percentage from 300g and re-multiplied to give the desired 1000g body butter.

Example 3

Assuming the body butter recipe was already in percentage (%) and you need to convert to grams for weighing. And we want to make
1000g body butter

Ingredient	Percentage (%)
Shea butter	20
Cocoa butter 16.7	
Mango butter	13.3
Moringa oil	10
Neem oil	6.7
Grape seed oil 33.3	

Solution 3

All standard recipes come in percentage as seen in example 3 but we must always convert back to weight for measurement

using equation
5.

Weight = $\frac{\text{Percentage} \times \text{Batch Size}}{100}$

Shea butter = 20/300 X 1000   = 200g

Cocoa butter= 16.7/300 X 1000   = 167g

3

Mango butter=13.3/300 X 1000 = 133g Moringa

oil=   10/300 X

1000   = 100g Neem

oil=   6.7/300 X 1000   = 67g

Grape seed oil =   33.3/300 X 1000   =
333g

Ingredient	Percentage (%)	g
Shea butter	20%	200g
Cocoa butter	16.7%	167g
Mango butter	13.3%	133g
Moringa oil	10%	100g
Neem oil	6.7%	67g
Grape seed oil 333g	33.3%	
Total	**100%**	**1000g**

From the above calculations we will need to measure out 200g, 167g,
133g, 100g, 67g and 333g of shea butter, cocoa butter, mango

butter, moringa oil, neem oil and grape seed oil respectively to make the body butter.

6.5 Measurement of Concentration

Sometimes, actives may be bought pre formulated and it is the formulator's duty to dilute further to suit specific use.

3

Conversion of Ingredient Concentration

Ca X Ga = Cb X Gb **Equation 6**

Where

Ca = Initial Concentration Cb =

Final Concentration Ga = Initial

Gram

Gb = Final Gram

For measurement of concentration, determine Ga (initial gram).

Example 4

You want to formulate a 5% glycolic acid toner of 100g. You buy glycolic acid and it is written 80% glycolic acid. The question is how many grams of glycolic acid do you need to measure out?

Solution 4

Ca = 80

Cb = 5

Ga = ?

Gb = 100

80 X ? = 5 X 100

? = 5 X 100/ 80   = 6.25g

So, instead of measuring 5g, you have to measure 6.25g to prevent systematic error.

3

CHAPTER SEVEN

7.0 PRESERVATION OF SKINCARE PRODUCTS

7.1 Skincare Products Preservation

Product preservation is an essential step in the formulation of skincare products. It involves the addition of antioxidants, preservatives and chelating agents to prevent spoilage due to microorganisms and oxidation. Spoilage of products leads to change in sensory properties, breakdown of emulsion, and can cause harm to the skin.

Three types of preservation are needed in skincare formulation: antioxidants, preservatives and chelating agents.

7.1.1 Antioxidants

Antioxidants are additives used to retard the formation of reactive oxygen species (ROS) leading to the oxidation of lipids (fats and oils). Lipids during storage break down in the presence of light, water, heat and/or metals to form ROS such as; peroxides and superoxides. The presence of these ROS in fats and oils gives an off odour known as **rancidity.** Antioxidants serve as free radical scavengers prolonging onset of oxidation and therefore keep lipids fresh for prolonged periods of time. Antioxidants used to prevent lipid oxidation must be oil soluble. Oil soluble antioxidants can be natural or synthetic. Most common and effective natural antioxidant is Vitamin E (Tocopherol). It is used at a percentage of 0.5-1% in the oil phase. Synthetic antioxidants are effective in lower concentration of 0.01 - 0.1%. Example includes: BHT (butylated hydroxytoluene) and BHA (butylated hydroxyanisole). Skincare products that have oils and fat as ingredient components must contain at least one type of the above antioxidants.

Apart from oil soluble antioxidants listed above, water soluble antioxidants are added to skincare products to prevent other antioxidants from oxidizing. Examples of antioxidants that need protection from oxidizing are: vitamin C, kojic acid, alpha arbutin,

3

phenolic antioxidants and glutathione. Common water soluble antioxidants used are; sodium metabisulphite, ferulic acid, rosemary extract and resveratrol. They are used in combination with oil soluble antioxidants for maximum protection of skin care products against oxidation.

7.1.2 Preservatives

Preservatives are water soluble additives used to prevent microbial spoilage of aqueous products. Any skincare formulation that requires the use of water, especially water in oil emulsions with pH within the range of 5 - 8 must contain one or more preservatives.

The choice of choosing the right preservative will depend largely on the pH of the final product and the ingredient composition. It is important to look out for incompatible ingredients especially when using organic acids. Also, it is important to note that most preservatives do not have a broad spectrum effect against Fungi, gram + and gram – Bacteria. Therefore, combination of preservatives is desirable. Table 4 serves as a guide in selecting appropriate preservatives for your formulated product.

It is important to note that the percentage usage in Table 4 is just a recommended value. It is also important to conduct a preservative challenge test for every preservative system and ensure the usage is within established standards in your country.

All preservatives should be dissolved in water and added to the cool down stage of formulation except otherwise stated by the manufacturer.

3

7.1.3 Chelating Agents

Chelating agents function as preservative stabilizers. They bind with heavy metals (metal ions) in water or other ingredients making these metals unavailable for chemical reactions that can lead to product spoilage. Chelators therefore play a crucial role in the stability and efficacy of skincare products.

According to INCI, chelating agents are defined as "ingredients that complex with and inactivate metallic ions to prevent their adverse effects on the stability or appearance of cosmetic products." The preservative effect of chelating agents is optimised when chelating agents are combined with antioxidants. Examples of natural chelating agents are amino acids such ethylenediamine and organic acids such as citric, phytic acid, lactic acid, gluconic acid and acetic acid.

Tetrasodium EDTA and disodium EDTA are example of synthetic chelating agents, As a rule of thumb, Tetrasodium EDTA is used for alkaline products (soaps and shampoos) while disodium EDTA is used for acidic products (creams, lotions, toners and serums). EDTA is used at concentration of 0.1 - 0.5%. The major setback of EDTA is it is not biodegradable thereby causing harm to the environment. Natural chelators are more environmentally friendly, however, they have selective effect in chelating some metal and are used at higher concentration from 0.5-4%.

In summary, to achieve maximum shelf stability of emulsions, skincare products should contain one or more antioxidants, a chelating agent and suitable broad spectrum preservative or preservatives combination.

3

Table 4: Choosing the Right Preservative

Preservative	% Usage	pH Stability	Activity	Safety
Organic Acids • Benzoic Acid/Sodium Benzoate • Sorbic Acid/Potassium sorbate • Levulinic Acid • Anisic Acid	0.5-1 < 0.6 < 0.3 < 0.3	3 – 6	Fungi	GRAS
Parabens • Germaben II • Methylparaben • Propylparaben • Butylparaben	0..1-0.3	Acidic medium	Fungi Gram +	Controversial estrogenic activity
Formaldehyde Releasers • Germall Plus • DMDM Hydantoin	0.1–0.5 <	pH Stable	Gram + and Gram – bacteria	Controversial estrogenic activity

• Imidazolidinyl Urea (IU) • Diazolidinyl Urea (DU)	0.6 < 0.6 0.2– 0.4			
Isothiazolinones • Kathon	0.1	pH stable	Broad spectru	GRAS

3

			m	
Phenoxyethanol • Optiphen • Optiphen Plus	1%	pH stable	Gram -	GRAS
Chelating Agents • Tetra/ DIsodium **EDTA** • Tetrahydroxypropy I Ethylenediamine • Phytic Acid/ Sodium phytate	0.1-0.2	pH Stable	-	GRAS

GRAS- Generally Regarded as Safe

7.2 Antimicrobial Efficacy Test

Antimicrobial efficacy testing (AET) is also known as preservative efficacy testing. It is a microbial challenge methodology used to ensure that the preservative in a product is sufficient to kill and prevent growth of microorganism over a specific period of time.

AET must be carried out at the final step of product development, before product launch to ensure customer safety during product usage. There are several types of AET but the most widely validated is the challenge test.

7.2.1 Challenge Test

Challenge test is used to ascertain the efficacy of preservatives over time. It involves inoculating a known amount of microorganism in a measured amount of product using its original packaging. The product is protected from light and incubated at room temperature for 28 days. The mortality rate is calculated and compared with the set standard.

3

A wide range of microorganisms is usually inoculated into the product, gram + cocci, gram- fermentative bacilli, gram- non-fermentative bacilli, yeast and mold. Collection of microorganisms usually consisting of, S. aureus, E. coli, P. aeruginosa, Candida albicans and Aspergillus niger. However, organisms known to pose a particular danger to a product type or organism harvested from a manufacturing environment may also be included.

Challenge Test Methodology

Step 1: Ascertain initial microbial load

Prior to the challenge test, the initial microbial load of the product should be determined. To ascertain initial microbial load, Standard Plate Count (SPC) of freshly prepared products should be determined according to, AOAC Official Method of Analysis, sec.
977.27. It is advised to conduct triplicate SPC on each product.

Step 2: Sample preparation

The product from the same batch as in Step 1, is packed into five containers, each being challenged by the 5 specified microorganisms stated above using the same packaging material intended for product marketing.

Step 3: Preservative challenge testing

The five containers will be inoculated with, S. aureus, E. coli, P. aeruginosa, Candida albicans and Aspergillus niger respectively.

Each of the microorganisms will have concentration of $>1 \times 10^5$ CFU/g or ml, which must be confirmed by standard dilution and plating techniques.

At the time of test initiation, a separate aliquot of the product (1g or

1ml) is added to neutralization broth that will be used later for product neutralization and recovery validation.

The inoculated samples are incubated at room temperature, away from light for no less than 28 days. Periodically (7, 14 and 28) days after inoculation, product samples are taken out for SPC to

3

determine the amount of microorganisms remaining.

Step 4: Report writing and interpretation

The log reduction of each microorganism at 7, 14 and 28 days is calculated and reported. The effectiveness of the preservative system is compared to accepted criteria ISO 11930.

The preservative challenge test must be carried out in a microbiology or pathology laboratory by experts. Doing it yourself is not encouraged.

7.3 Antioxidant Efficacy Test

Antioxidant efficacy test is a voluntary test to ensure that the oils and fats in a formulation have not been broken down into ROS. The test conducted is accelerated oxidation test such as oxidative stability index and schaal oven test and swift stability test. It is mostly beneficial in high fat content skin care products such as glow oils, cleansing oils/balms and body butters.

Antioxidant efficacy test involves placing a known amount of fatty product in an elevated temperature (50 – 200°C) with excess air flow over a period of time to determine the induction period of oxidation. Common parameters measured are peroxide value, conductivity, anisidine value and fatty acid composition.

Antioxidant efficacy tests must be carried out by chemists. Doing it yourself is dangerous because analysis requires the use of toxic chemicals and sophisticated equipment.

3

Made in United States
Troutdale, OR
01/20/2024

17028287R00064